The Magic School Bus
Inside the Human Body

By Joanna Cole   Illustrated by Bruce Degen

Hippo

The author and illustrator wish to thank Dr Arnold J Capute, Associate Professor of Pediatrics, Director, Division of Child Development, Johns Hopkins University School of Medicine, for his assistance in preparing this book.

Scholastic Children's Books,
Commonwealth House, 1-19 New Oxford Street,
London WC1A 1NU, UK
a division of Scholastic Ltd
London ~ New York ~ Toronto ~ Sydney ~ Auckland

First published in the US by Scholastic Inc.
This edition published by Scholastic Ltd, 1996

Text copyright © Joanna Cole, 1989
Illustrations © Bruce Degen, 1989

ISBN: 0 590 13950 9

10 9 8 7 6 5 4

The right of Joanna Cole and Bruce Degen to be identified as the author and illustrator respectively of this work has been asserted by them in accordance with the Copyright, Designs and Patents Act, 1988.

THE MAGIC SCHOOL BUS is a trademark of Scholastic Inc.

To Craig
from Joanna
& Bruce

It all began when Miss Frizzle
showed our class a film strip
about the human body.
We all knew trouble was about to start,
because we knew Miss Frizzle
was the strangest teacher in the school.

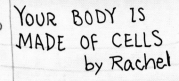

YOUR BODY IS MADE OF CELLS
by Rachel

Your body seems to be all one piece, but actually it is made of trillions of tiny pieces, called cells.

MY BODY IS MADE OF TRILLIONS OF CELLS.

SO IS MINE!

The very next day, The Friz made us do an experiment on our own bodies.

SEE YOUR OWN CELLS

Most cells are so small that we can't see them without a microscope.

① Gently scrape inside of cheek with toothpick

② Stir end of toothpick in drop of water on a slide.

③ Add a drop of Iodine Solution to colour cells.

④ Look at slide under microscope. See your cells.

OOOH, WEIRD!

Then she announced that we were going on a class trip to the science museum. We were going to see an exhibit about how our bodies get energy from the food we eat.

YOUR CELLS NEED ENERGY TO HELP YOU GROW, MOVE, TALK, THINK, AND PLAY.

Jail Cell →

JUST BEING IN MS. FRIZZLE'S CLASS TAKES ALL MY ENERGY.

DIFFERENT KINDS OF CELLS HAVE DIFFERENT JOBS
by Gregory

Lung cells help you breathe.

Muscle Cells help you move.

ODE TO JELLY

Brain Cells help you think.

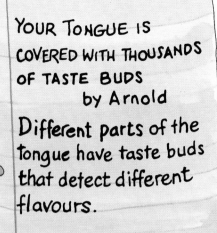

BITTER

SOUR

SALT

SWEET

The trip started out like any other trip.
We rode to the museum
in the old school bus.
Along the way,
we stopped at a park for lunch.

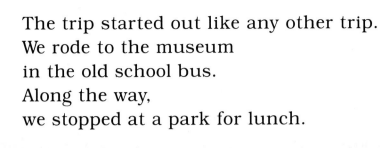

LEFT OVER
FISH FINGERS?!
ICK!

I'LL SWOP YOU THESE
TERRIFIC FISH FINGERS
FOR THAT HORRIBLE
PEANUT BUTTER AND
BANANA SANDWICH.

FORGET IT!

TAKE A LOOK
AT HER SHOES.

PLEASE!
I'M EATING!

When it was time to go,
everyone got back on the bus—
everyone but Arnold.
He was still at the picnic table,
daydreaming and eating
a bag of Cheesie-Weesies.

WHEN YOU EAT, YOUR BODY DIGESTS THE FOOD SO YOUR CELLS CAN USE IT TO MAKE ENERGY.

YOUR BODY NEEDS GOOD FOOD
by Carmen
For high energy and good growing power eat lots of:

Fresh fruits and Vegetables

Milk and Milk products

Whole grain cereal and Pasta

Lean Meats, Fish, Poultry, AND eggs

AND NOT TOO MUCH JUNK FOOD!

A SCIENCE WORD
by Dorothy Ann

Digestion comes from a word that means to divide. When food is digested it is divided into smaller and smaller parts.

"Hurry up, Arnold!" called Miss Frizzle. She reached for the ignition key, but instead she pushed a strange little button nearby.

At once, we started shrinking and spinning through the air.

From inside, we couldn't see what was happening. All we knew was that we landed suddenly...

and then we were going down a dark tunnel.
We had no idea where we were.
But, as usual, Miss Frizzle knew.
She said we were inside a human body,
going down the oesophagus—
the tube that leads from the throat
to the stomach.
Most of us were too upset
about leaving Arnold behind
to pay much attention.

WHERE'S ARNOLD?

HE GOT LEFT!

THAT'S WHAT HAPPENS WHEN YOU EAT JUNK FOOD!

I THOUGHT WE WERE GOING TO THE MUSEUM.

THERE'S BEEN A SLIGHT CHANGE OF PLANS... WE'RE BEING DIGESTED INSTEAD.

FOOD GOES TO YOUR STOMACH THROUGH THE OESOPHAGUS
by Wanda
The food does not just fall down.
It is pushed along by muscle actions the way toothpaste is squeezed out of a tube. That's why you can swallow even when you are upside down.

MUSCLES SQUEEZE TO PUSH FOOD TO YOUR STOMACH

WHY ARE THE INTESTINES
COILED UP?
by John

In an adult the intestines are 7.5 metres (25 feet) long. If they were stretched out straight, a person would have to be as tall as a house.

STOMACH

FOOD GOES FROM THE STOMACH TO THE SMALL INTESTINE

WASTE GOES OUT THROUGH THE LARGE INTESTINE

The small intestine was
a coiled-up hollow tube.
The inner walls of the tube were covered
with tiny "fingers" called *villi*.
"In the *villi* are tiny blood vessels.
Food molecules are taken into
these blood vessels,"
said Miss Frizzle.
"Once the food is in the blood,
it can travel all over the body."

We felt ourselves getting even smaller,
and Miss Frizzle started driving
into one of the *villi*.
She was going straight into a blood vessel!

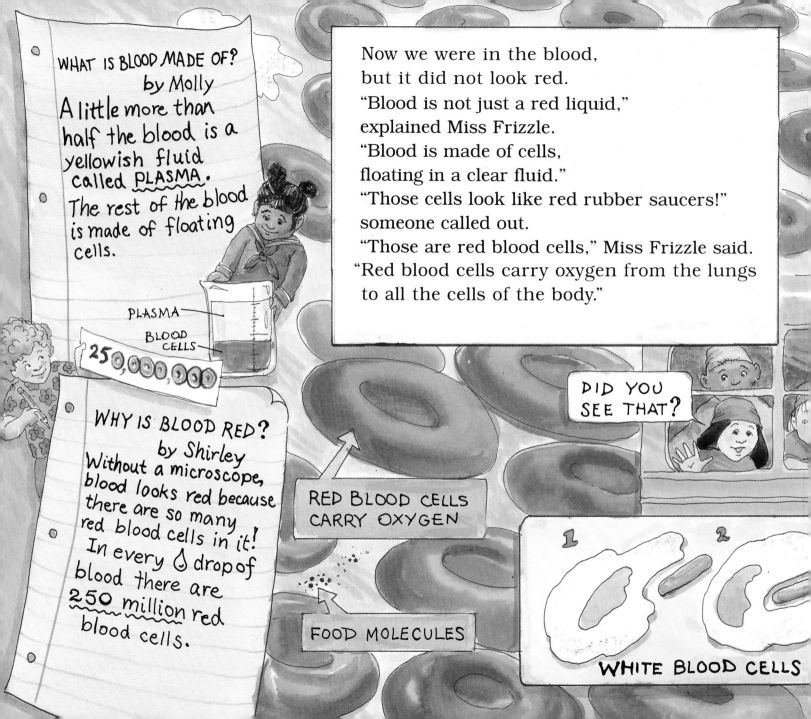

Looking back, we saw a white blood cell
chasing the bus.
"We'll be safer with the red blood cells, kids,"
said Miss Frizzle.
She reached for the handle
that controlled the bus's doors.
Don't do it!" we cried,
but when did Miss Frizzle ever listen?
The doors of the bus flew open.

THAT WHITE BLOOD
CELL MUST THINK
THE SCHOOL BUS
IS A GERM.

WELL, THE BUS
IS PRETTY DIRTY.

We were swept out of the bus
and into the bloodstream.
"Everybody hitch a ride!" called The Friz.
Each kid grabbed a red blood cell
as it went by.
Our last glimpse of the bus
was when it went into another blood vessel—
with the white blood cell right behind it!

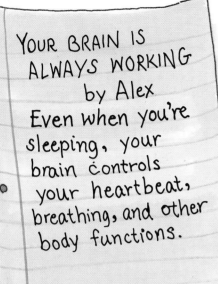

YOUR BRAIN IS ALWAYS WORKING
by Alex
Even when you're sleeping, your brain controls your heartbeat, breathing, and other body functions.

When we reached the brain, we let go of our red blood cells and squeezed out of the blood vessel. It was hard to believe that this wrinkled grey blob was the control centre of the body.

YOUR BRAIN NEVER LIES DOWN ON THE JOB.

3:00 A.M. and still at it.

CHILDREN, WE ARE WALKING ON THE CEREBRAL CORTEX, THE PINKISH GREY, OUTER LAYER OF THE BRAIN. WITHOUT IT WE COULDN'T SEE, HEAR, SMELL, TOUCH, TASTE, TALK, MOVE, OR THINK!

CEREBRAL CORTEX
Controls thinking, moving and the five senses.

MOTOR CENTRE (TELLS MUSCLES TO MOVE)

SPEECH CENTRE

HEARING CENTRE

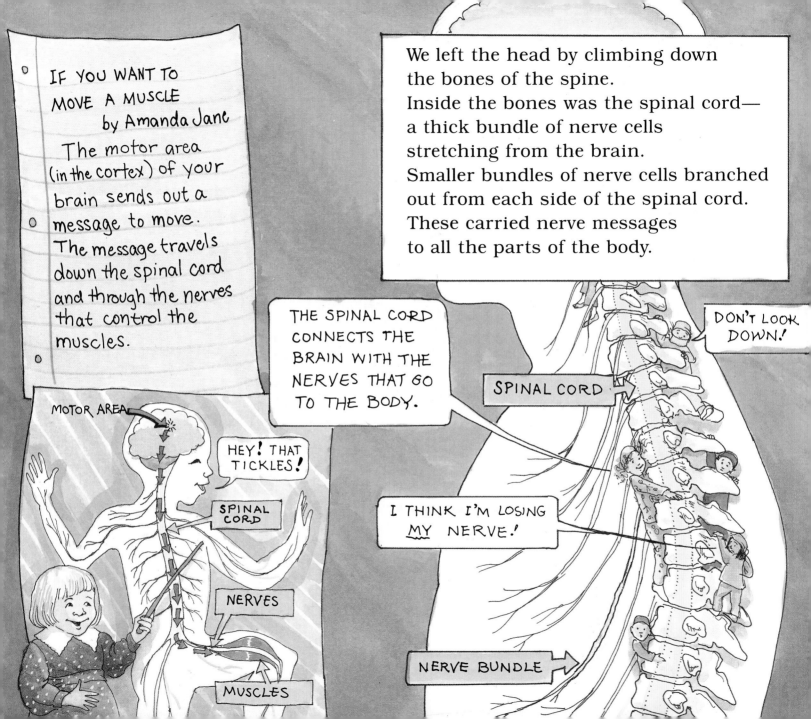

We followed some nerves that went to the leg muscles.
The leg muscles were working hard.
They needed a lot of energy.
They used up a lot of food and oxygen from the blood.
The heart was beating faster to carry fresh blood to the muscle cells.

We entered a nearby blood vessel.
The blood was moving so fast,
we were afraid we would
lose each other.
But at that moment,
the school bus floated by.
What a relief!
We jumped on and went up
through the heart and lungs again—
just the way we went before.

When we emerged from the bloodsteam,
we were in a huge open space.
"Where are we?" asked a kid.
Miss Frizzle explained,
"Children, this is the nasal cavity,"
"The what?" we asked.
"The inside of the nose," said The Friz.
Suddenly, we heard a deafening noise.
It sounded like "Ah-aa-aa-ah!"

A tremendous blast of air
hit the bus full force.
We flew forward,
spinning round and round.

CHILDREN, PREPARE FOR LANDING. PLEASE REMAIN SEATED UNTIL THE SCHOOL BUS HAS COME TO A COMPLETE STOP.

IS SHE FOR REAL?

A-A-A-AH CHOO!

BLESS YOU!

"Arnold!" we said, "the trip was *amazing!* You should have been there!"

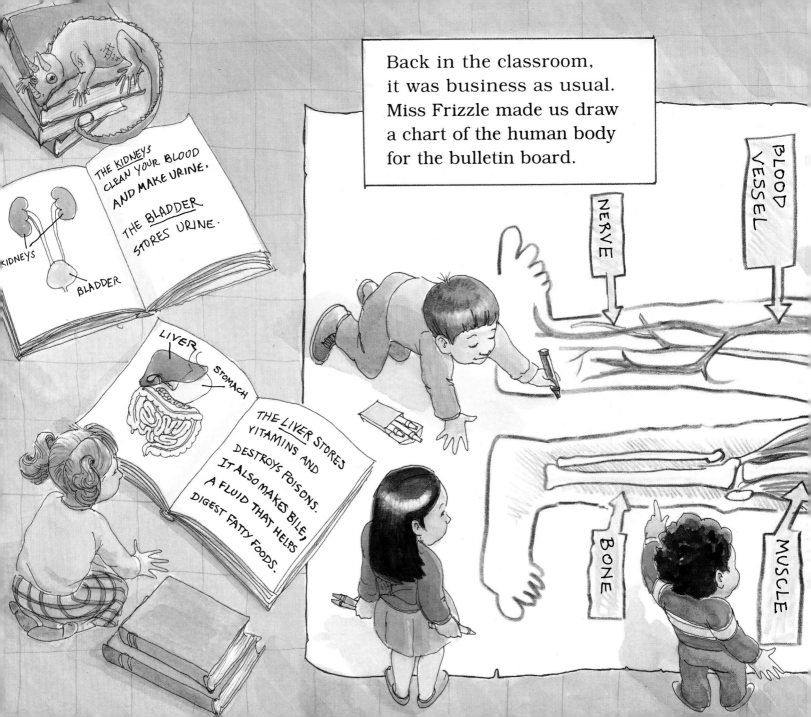

Back in the classroom,
it was business as usual.
Miss Frizzle made us draw
a chart of the human body
for the bulletin board.

THE KIDNEYS CLEAN YOUR BLOOD AND MAKE URINE.

THE BLADDER STORES URINE.

KIDNEYS

BLADDER

LIVER

STOMACH

THE LIVER STORES VITAMINS AND DESTROYS POISONS. IT ALSO MAKES BILE, A FLUID THAT HELPS DIGEST FATTY FOODS.

NERVE

BLOOD VESSEL

BONE

MUSCLE

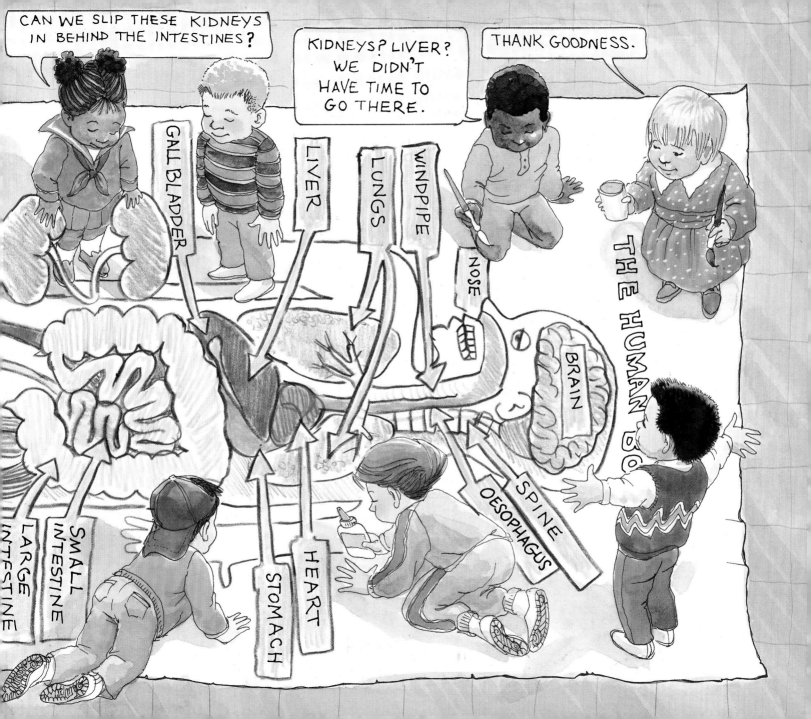

TRUE-OR-FALSE TEST

STOP! TAKE THIS TEST!
DO NOT WATCH T.V. ... YET.
DO NOT GET A SNACK ... YET.
DO NOT PLAY A VIDEO
GAME ... YET.

FIRST TAKE THIS TEST.

HOW TO:
Read the sentences below. Decide if each one is true or false. To see if you are correct, check the answers on the opposite page.

QUESTIONS:

1. A school bus can enter someone's body and kids can go on a tour. True or false?

2. Museums are boring. True or false?

3. Arnold should not have tried to get back to school by himself. True or false?

4. Children cannot breathe or talk when they are surrounded by a liquid. True or false?

5. If the children really were as small as cells, we couldn't see them without a microscope. True or false?

6. White blood cells actually chase and destroy disease germs. True or false?

7. Miss Frizzle really knew where Arnold was the whole time. True or false?

ANSWERS:

1. False! That could not happen in real life. (Not even to Arnold.)

   But in this story the author had to make it happen. Otherwise, the book would have been about a trip to a museum, instead of a trip through the body.

2. False! Museums are interesting and fun. But they are not as strange and gross as actually going inside a human body.

3. True! In real life, it would have been safer if Arnold had found a police officer to help.

4. True. If children were *really* inside a blood vessel, they would drown. It must have been magic.

5. True! The pictures in this book show the cells and the children greatly enlarged.

6. True! As unbelievable as it seems, real white blood cells actually behave just like the ones in this book. They even squeeze through the cells of blood vessel walls to capture germs in your organs and tissues.

7. Probably true. No one is absolutely sure, but most people think Miss Frizzle knows *everything*.